Cua

Wrestling
Greats

HAYSTACKS
CALHOUN

Ross Davies

The Rosen Publishing Group, Inc.
New York

Published in 2001 by The Rosen Publishing Group, Inc.
29 East 21st Street, New York, NY 10010

Copyright © 2001 by The Rosen Publishing Group, Inc.

First Edition

Library of Congress Cataloging-in-Publication Data

Davies, Ross.
Haystacks Calhoun / by Ross Davies.— 1st ed.
p. cm.— (Wrestling greats)
Includes bibliographical references (p.) and index.
ISBN 0-8239-3435-7 (lib. bdg.)
1. Calhoun, Haystacks, 1934–1989—Juvenile literature. 2. Wrestlers—United States—Biography—Juvenile literature. [1. Calhoun, Haystacks, 1934–1989. 2. Wrestlers.] I. Title.
GV1196.C35 D38 2001
796.812'092—dc21

2001000178

Manufactured in the United States of America

Contents

Larger-than-life wrestling legend Haystacks Calhoun endeared himself to millions of fans.

"My Size Has Made Me a Lonely Man"

Heads turned. The giant-sized man walked down the Manhattan street on a weekday afternoon. Those he passed couldn't help but turn and stare. They were giving their full attention to one of the biggest men they had ever seen! Though each passerby thought that the object of his or her staring was unaware of the open-mouthed, unabashed looks, he did know. Haystacks Calhoun always knew.

"I'm six feet four inches and weigh 601 pounds, and I'm used to people looking at me funny."

"But I'm not a curiosity," Haystacks would think to himself. "I'm just an ol' country boy who likes scufflin'. I'm just like everyone else."

Walking down that street that day in 1965, Haystacks wasn't like everyone else at all—he was three times the size of most people, sticking out like a sore thumb. While everyone else was wearing suits and business clothes, he was wearing custom-made blue overalls (flown in from Oshkosh, Wisconsin) and a blue denim shirt that was big enough to cover a queen-sized bed. The shirt barely wrapped around his twenty-five-inch neck and his twenty-three-inch biceps.

Haystacks was also wearing sandals instead of shoes—it was hard to find size 12EEEEE shoes at the local store. He wore a horseshoe around his neck attached to a chain that, if he took it off, would wrap around three bicycles. And Haystacks had a full growth of dark, black beard because he hadn't shaved since the day he was able to.

There was another difference between Haystacks and other people: They were working nine to five and going home on the subway; Haystacks, on the other hand, was going to be working that night at Madison Square Garden, the most famous arena in the United States. Haystacks was a professional wrestler, and that night his audience would consist of over 15,000 people, all of whom would scream his name and act like they loved him.

Although everybody was watching him, and Haystacks was walking the streets of the most populated city in the United States, he felt all alone, like he was an outcast. Then again, he had always felt like that.

"I'm six feet four inches and weigh 601 pounds, and I'm used to people looking at me funny."

-Haystacks Calhoun

As a child, Haystacks was made fun of. The other kids used to laugh and call him "fat boy." Later in life, he would walk up to ticket windows at the airport and be told that he had to buy two tickets because of his size. He was turned away by one wrestling promoter after another—they all thought he was too fat to wrestle. Even when Haystacks finally convinced one promoter to give him a chance, he was treated like a circus sideshow act. "SPECIAL ADDED ATTRACTION!" the promotional poster read, as though he was something to be gawked at, like the bearded woman or the man with two heads.

In New York City, Haystacks Calhoun felt alone. He had been recently divorced from his first wife, and he longed for a home-cooked meal. Few restaurants could

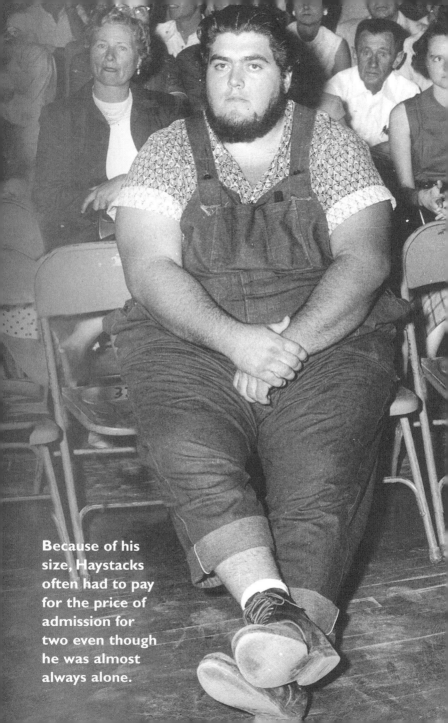

Because of his size, Haystacks often had to pay for the price of admission for two even though he was almost always alone.

meet his demands (and eating three or four entrées could get pretty expensive). He wanted there to be someone who would meet him when he came home from a long wrestling trip. He needed somebody to hug, somebody to talk to. But he didn't have anybody.

While life in the big city was lonely, life on the long road was even lonelier. Traveling in his customized station wagon, with the driver's seat twice the size of a normal one, Haystacks often talked to himself—after all, there was nobody else to talk to. This habit made him even more of a curiosity. People would drive past and see a very big man talking to himself. That made them stare even harder. One day, Haystacks broke a hotel bed. It was just too small and flimsy to hold his gigantic frame. He hung his head in shame as he explained what happened to the hotel clerk.

Haystacks kept on wondering why people didn't understand. He wondered how people could be so cruel. But most of all, he wondered if he would ever escape from his body—this prison that had become his life sentence.

"All big people live in a sort of lonely world, a world all to themselves," Haystacks told a magazine interviewer. "For some strange reason, people are afraid of me. People look at me as if I was some sort of freak or something. Fear is a strong emotion and it's difficult to overcome.

"My size seems to make people afraid. They stare at me and wonder how much I weigh. Even wrestling fans look at me in awe. You know, I love little kids, but most of 'em stay away from me. I guess that's really the biggest problem I face. My size has made me a lonely man."

Haystacks kept on walking down Broadway, trying to ignore the stares, hoping that one of these people would send a friendly glance his way, but knowing that none of them would. He knew what it was like to be the loneliest man in the world.

The Son of a Dirt Farmer

Texas is one of the biggest states in the union, so it's appropriate that one of the biggest men in wrestling history was born there.

William D. Calhoun was born on August 3, 1934, in McKinney, Texas. He was unusual from the second he came out of his mother's belly. The son of Denman Calhoun and Mittie Hayes Calhoun, William weighed a whopping eleven and three-quarters pounds at birth.

The Calhouns never had much money. McKinney, where they lived in northern Texas, was famous for its black earth. William's father owned a dirt farm, but the money from the farm barely covered the bills. As William got older and bigger, he discovered that he didn't mind the life of the Texas dirt farmer. He didn't have many friends, and he was an only child, so he spent a lot of time with his parents. Doing chores on the farm was fine because he could lose himself in his work.

William had attentive parents. Before and

Haystacks weighed 11 3/4 pounds at birth!

after school, and during the hot Texas summers, he would work on the farm with his father. At lunch and dinnertime, Mittie Hayes Calhoun would make huge meals for her two men.

"It wasn't an accident that I growed as big as I am," Haystacks told *Wrestling World* magazine in 1965. "My ma wouldn't hold still less'n I ate every bite on my plate and I liked her cookin' so much, I wouldn't quit as long as there was a morsel left on the table. Ma kept fixin' more every meal so that her little boy wouldn't go away hungry and I kept at eatin' more every meal so none of Ma's good vittles would go to waste."

At that time, with the United States coming out of the Great Depression, wasting food was a sin. Food and money were hard to come by. Because of this, and because of his large size, young William never let a morsel go to waste.

The Calhouns eventually moved to Pleasant Grove, Texas, where William became more of an outcast than before. It's one thing to be a fat kid in a place where you've lived all your life. It's even worse to be a fat kid in a new place. By the time he was a teenager, William weighed 500 pounds. William was incredibly strong, and he worked on a hay farm during the summers. William could load two stacks of hay—weighing seventy-five pounds each—for every one that the other workers loaded.

"The other men used to be mad at me because I could do twice as much work as they could in half the amount of time," Calhoun said. "Back then, we got paid by how much we loaded, not by how much time we worked, so I was making twice as much as everybody else. That made my Ma and Pop real happy because money wasn't easy to come by, and I weighed a whole heckuva lot."

William Calhoun wasn't a complete outcast. He had some friends, although not any really close ones. Together, they often wrestled for fun. At 400 pounds, Calhoun could have easily beaten any of them, so he occasionally would take on three, four, five, or six kids at a time. This turned out to be good training for Calhoun's wrestling career, especially in battle royals—free-for-alls involving twenty or more wrestlers—which Calhoun always won. The key is to dump your opponents over the top rope and be the last man standing. As a teenager, William was always the last man standing.

At school, William Calhoun was a joke. He was the subject of constant teasing, all because of his size. One day he overheard the other boys in the locker room calling him a freak. "Hey Calhoun! Fat boy! Did you ever see your shoes?" the mean kids would taunt him.

"I didn't feel like no freak," Calhoun said years later." Maybe once in a while I'd look in the mirror and say to myself, `Now why the heck are you so big?' but other than my size, I didn't think I was different from anyone else. But then I heard those kids talkin' about me, and I went home and asked my Ma, `Ma, am I a freak?'"

William's parents tried to reassure him, but they were of average size and couldn't understand what he was going through. Only one person could truly sympathize with William—his Aunt Clara, who weighed 510 pounds.

"You can't get angry at those people, William," she would tell him." You've got to feel sorry for them. It's a terrible thing to look at a person and see only what's on the outside. Because of their handicap, many of them will never get to know what a fine young man you are. They'll be missing a chance to make a true friend. They're the real freaks."

"Now why the heck are you so big?"

-William Calhoun
(to himself)

William's conversation with his aunt was a turning point in his life. He could have lashed out at the people who made fun of him. He could have turned around and called them freaks, too. Even worse, because he was so big, he easily could have beaten them up on the playground or after school, just to teach them a lesson.

   But William Calhoun decided to teach his detractors a different kind of lesson, a lesson in how to be nice to people. Rather than doing to others what they were doing to him, William realized that his best course of action was to set a good example. It was best to be kind to everyone else, because he knew exactly how it felt when people weren't kind to him.

   "There ain't no reason to make people feel bad," William decided. He would live by that hard-learned rule for the rest of his life.

3 "Just Give Me a Chance, Mister!"

What can a 385-pound, fourteen-year-old boy do? Well, he can certainly play football, and that's just what William Calhoun did when he started high school in Pleasant Grove, Texas.

William was a formidable foe for rival players and teams. He played defensive guard (he wasn't fast enough to play offense) and dominated games with his size and strength. Opponents would double- and triple-team him, but to no avail. Using his mind, as well as his size, William devised a strategy that, to this day, has never been copied. When the ball was hiked, he would charge into the center. Just as the quarterback handed the ball off to the fullback, William would knock the center back into the fullback to break up the play. He was tackling the ball handler without even touching him!

William was a natural on the football field. Unlike the other players, he didn't even have to work out.

"I don't go around picking up barbells because, between you and me, I'm too lazy," he said at the time. "But I can lift my weight, and when I worked the farm, I picked up whatever had to be picked up."

There was no way William could realize it at the time, but he was already in training to become a professional wrestler. His calm, friendly demeanor, which he displayed even when he was being taunted, would eventually make him one of the most beloved wrestlers ever. His ferocity on the football field and his charges into the offensive center would one day be duplicated in his across-the-ring charges at opponents.

During the cold Texas winters, the Calhoun family kept the house warm by burning a fire in the fireplace. Electric heat was a rarity back then, and gas heat was simply too expensive. William's job was to break kindling wood for the fire. If the wood was too thick to break with his hands, he'd jump on it with his stomach. Crack! William had developed a new and effective way to break wood. Later on, he used this same move to squash opponents in the ring.

During the long, hot, Texas summers, Calhoun often went swimming in a wide, deep creek near his house. "I noticed that whenever I jumped in the creek, I knocked all the water out," Calhoun said, exaggerating only slightly.

William's weight, however, continued to be a problem, at least as far as his parents and doctors were concerned.

"I always felt fine," Haystacks recalled. "When I was fourteen, a doctor told me I was going to die any day. But I'll probably outlive him. I've been a guinea pig for hospitals all over the country. I've been to doctors' conventions and they've poked at me and prodded and then told me I didn't have a glandular condition or anything, that my organs were big enough to stand the strain. They would run these tests and look at me and say, `You're just plain big, period.'"

William Calhoun tried to convince himself that he was "just plain big, period," but other doctors were telling him that he was on the verge of death. One can only imagine what it's like to be a perfectly healthy fourteen-year-old boy and have doctors say that there's something wrong with you and you're probably not going to make it to fifteen. Meanwhile, William tried to lose weight, but he just couldn't do it.

He defied the doctors and celebrated his fifteenth, sixteenth, seventeenth and eighteenth birthdays! By the age of eighteen, he weighed 450 pounds!

After graduating from high school, William hoped to play college football. Unfortunately, at the time, the top college teams in the country did not use a platoon system—meaning that they used the same players on offense and defense, rather than using different players for when they had the ball and when they didn't have the ball. William was a standout defensive guard, but he wasn't good enough or mobile enough to play offensive guard. Because of this, his college football career ended before it even started.

Next, William turned to his second love. Growing up, he had loved watching wrestling matches on television. The late 1940s and early 1950s were the glory days of televised pro wrestling. In fact, back then wrestling was one of the few shows being broadcast on television. As more and more people bought black-and-white televisions, the popularity of wrestling increased in the United States. William loved watching Gorgeous George, Buddy Rogers, Lou Thesz, and

Lou Thesz was one of young William Calhoun's favorite
wrestlers during the late '40s and early '50s.

Whipper William Watson on his parents' tiny television set.

The wrestlers he was watching were huge and strong, but William realized that he was huge and strong, too.

"I can do this!" he told himself.

In 1952, William packed his bags, said good-bye to his parents and his dear Aunt Clara, and took a bus to Dallas.

"Just gimme a chance," William told the first promoter he met.

But the promoter wasn't interested.

"I'm not running a circus," the man told him.

William thanked the man for his time and moved on. He went from town to town and was turned down by a half dozen more promoters. William was running out of money and patience. He didn't have a job, and there was no way he could last much longer on what he had in his pocket. Then, one day, William heard about a promoter in Kansas City named Orville Brown. Brown

The exploits of '40s wrestlers like Whipper William Watson inspired William Calhoun to become a professional wrestler.

was a former world champion and from what William heard, he was a good guy.

"He might turn me down," he thought, "but maybe he won't insult me like the others did."

William scraped together enough money to buy a bus ticket to Kansas City, realizing that this could be his last chance. When he arrived in Kansas City, he felt the same way he did when he was anywhere else—like a freak. But Orville Brown, a shrewd man, saw great potential in him.

"I'll work with you," Brown said, even though he was concerned that William didn't have any mat experience. "I'm going to make you into a wrestler. It'll be hard work and there'll be times you'll want to forget it. But if you do, I'll understand."

"Don't worry about that, neighbor," said William. "I've never wanted anything as much in my whole life."

William was true to his word. He worked harder than he ever had in his entire life. Day after day, straining and sweating, he practiced holds in the gym. After each four-hour training session, William would drag his big body back to the hotel and flop down on his bed. One day, much to his horror, the bed broke.

William was far away from Texas, and he was getting homesick. He missed his mother and father. But he couldn't quit. After all, he didn't want to spend the rest of his life working on a dirt farm. So William stayed in Kansas City and trained for six months. Sometimes, the torture of the training sessions was unbearable, but he felt himself getting stronger and more confident. And William was learning about being a professional wrestler.

Finally, after an especially difficult training session, Orville Brown walked up to William and said, "You're ready. You're wrestling next week."

William could hardly believe what he was hearing. All of the rejection and hard work had been worth it. He was finally about to become a professional wrestler.

As Big as a Haystack

few days later, Orville Brown showed William a promotional poster for the upcoming weekend's wrestling card. In big letters, it read, "SPECIAL ADDED ATTRACTION. IN HIS PROFESSIONAL DEBUT—COUNTRY BOY CALHOUN!"

William wasn't sure how he felt about this. One thing he did like was his new name—Country Boy Calhoun. It sounded good. He certainly was a country boy, but William wasn't so sure about being an "attraction." He had never thought of himself as an attraction and certainly never liked it when people stared at him. William worried that people would view him as a curiosity and would come to see him only because of his size. Fortunately, the poster made no mention of his weight.

Although William wasn't quite sure if he should laugh or cry, he was certainly thrilled. The night before his first match, he could barely sleep. He tossed and turned, and the bedsprings squeaked and groaned under his 450 pounds, just as he hoped his opponent would groan under his weight the following day.

"Well," he thought, "I know one thing for sure, I'm gonna be a heckuva lot bigger than whoever it is I'm wrestling."

The next night in Kansas City, Country Boy Calhoun walked into the ring wearing a T-shirt, overalls, and his father's horseshoe around his neck. The fans didn't know what to think. Calhoun's opponent was Lou Plummer, an experienced wrestler about half his size.

When the bell rang to start the match, Plummer bumped him in the stomach. Calhoun didn't budge. He hadn't felt anything. Calhoun grabbed Plummer around the neck and applied downward pressure to his head. Plummer tried to back off, but Calhoun kept moving after him. When they got to the ropes, the referee forced the two wrestlers to release. Plummer's face was red, and sweat was pouring down his face. Meanwhile, Calhoun wasn't even breathing hard.

Plummer got desperate. He bounced off the ropes and tried to hit Calhoun with a cross-body block. Calhoun took three steps to the side, and Plummer hit nothing but air. He landed flat on his face. The crowd laughed.

"They're laughing with me," Calhoun realized, much to his delight.

Calhoun went in for the kill. He placed Plummer in a headlock and twisted his body as if it were a rag doll. Then he pushed Plummer to the ropes, executed his giant splash, and scored the pin. The entire match took three minutes! When Calhoun walked back to the locker room, the crowd was cheering.

"I've been scufflin' since I was five," Calhoun told the reporters who surrounded his locker after the match. "I had to because I've always been big and folks like to pick on me. But they leave me alone after I fall on them."

"What about your weight?" a reporter asked.

"What about it?" Calhoun replied.

"Isn't it a problem?" another reporter inquired.

"I tried to lose weight when I was young, but I couldn't lose a pound. My

When he was a kid, people made fun of Haystacks because of his girth, but as a wrestler, his size made him a success.

weight isn't a problem to me, nor is it a comfort."

"What's it like to be so big," asked one reporter.

"What's it like to be small?" Calhoun replied. "You tell me—I wouldn't know. I've always been big."

Later that night, Calhoun decided he no longer wanted to be known by his birth name "because William Calhoun sounds too much like a guy who signed the Declaration of Independence." Country Boy Calhoun was just fine.

Word spread quickly about the 450-pound wrestler who moved like a man half his size and could squash opponents with his giant splashes. Within months, Country

Boy Calhoun had become a major success in Kansas City. One night, a television announcer asked him what made him tick.

"Neighbor," Calhoun said, "I'm just an ol' country boy who likes scufflin'. I never scuffled in any organized competition before, but me and a few of the boys used to do some scufflin' out behind the barn. I just was fortunate enough to discover that scufflin' is what I do best."

Calhoun realized that his size made him unique. If he had weighed 200 pounds, it would have taken him a lot longer to attract so much attention. On the other hand, if he weighed 200 pounds, he could have played college football, and the promoters in Texas wouldn't have turned him away so quickly. For the first time in his life, Calhoun's size was an asset.

All of a sudden, promoters around the United States wanted him to wrestle on their cards. In the late 1950s, Washington, DC, was the wrestling capital of the United States. If a wrestler could make it there, he could make it anywhere. One day, Calhoun received a phone call from a promoter on the East Coast. The promoter wanted him to wrestle in the nation's capital.

"I'm just an ol' country boy who likes scufflin'."

-Haystacks Calhoun

To get from Kansas City to Washington, DC, Calhoun had to fly on a plane for the first time in his life. Unfortunately for Calhoun, the woman at the ticket counter wasn't very understanding. She told him that he would have to buy two tickets because he was so big, he couldn't possibly take up only one seat. Fortunately, a midget wrestler friend of Calhoun's was along for the trip.

"I assume," Calhoun's friend said, "that since he has to pay double, I only have to pay half fare."

"Of course not," the manager said. "You must pay full fare."

"Well, if he has to pay double because he's twice the size, then I should

Haystacks Calhoun puts the Bruiser in a bear hug in Cincinnati in May 1961.

pay only half because I'm only half the size of a regular passenger."

The woman gave in, although the armrest had to be removed from Calhoun's seat so that he could fit.

As soon as the plane arrived in Washington, Calhoun dropped off his stuff at the hotel and went sightseeing. The famous monuments amazed him. He wrote a letter to his parents, telling them about the Lincoln Memorial and the White House. This was big stuff for a dirt farmer from Texas! Calhoun felt like he had really hit the big time.

The next day, Calhoun walked into the office of promoter Vince McMahon. He was the most important promoter on the

East Coast (his son, Vince McMahon Jr., is now the owner of the World Wrestling Federation). McMahon took one look at Calhoun, gasped, and said, "You're as big as a haystack! Make that two haystacks!"

Calhoun had never heard it put that way before, but he didn't mind. Later, while McMahon was typing out the program inserts that listed the matches for the card, he couldn't remember Calhoun's first name. With no time to waste, McMahon typed "Haystacks Calhoun."

The card that night was nationally televised. Haystacks Calhoun won his match easily. Suddenly, everybody knew about the friendly wrestler who was as big as a haystack.

5 Making the Big Time

s the legend of Haystacks Calhoun spread across the country, William Calhoun grew, too. By 1958, he was 6'4" and weighed 600 pounds. Haystacks had discovered that the more he ate and the bigger he got, the more effective he was in the wrestling ring. Being big didn't slow him down, but it certainly made him a more imposing ring opponent.

Haystacks had no trouble finding work. He wrestled five nights a week up and down the East Coast. He bought a customized station wagon with rein-forced shock absorbers. After losing to Calhoun in Montréal, Frank Valois exclaimed, "You haven't really been bodyslammed until you've been body-slammed by Haystacks."

In Houston, Texas, one night, wrestler Art Neilson slugged Haystacks over the back of the head with a wood board. Haystacks complained that Neilson should have been disqualified.

"You should be fined or barred from Texas," Haystacks said.

"Don't talk that way to me, you sack of lard," responded Neilson, "or I'll toss you on your anterior."

Haystacks retorted, "I'll bet you a hundred bucks that you couldn't toss me on my anterior or posterior the longest day you live."

Before Neilson and Haystacks could go at it right then and there, the promoter leaped between them and said, "Wait, fellas, if you hurt any of these people you'll have me closed up like a Broadway theater! Why don't you both come back next week and throw each other out of the ring? That way, we'll all get paid for it, and we won't get me closed up."

"We'll do it, won't we, you big sack of lard?" Neilson screamed at Haystacks.

Haystacks just nodded. He realized there was no use saying another word.

Besides, he weighed 640 pounds. Neilson weighed 240 pounds. Neilson couldn't even lift him.

The next week, Neilson tried every trick in the book to knock Haystacks to the floor. He tried a hiplock but couldn't budge him. Finally, after eleven minutes of complete frustration, Neilson was in perfect position while Haystacks was off balance. He grabbed Haystacks around the neck and flipped him over. The whole ring shook when Haystacks landed. Haystacks was stunned. Neilson had won his hundred dollars.

Haystacks became an international sensation. In February 1960, Haystacks was wrestling in Florida when a representative of Fidel Castro's Cuban government invited him to wrestle in Havana, Cuba. Haystacks accepted the invitation.

"I was received royally," Haystacks recalled. "I was met by a group of Castro's agents, and it was like a Broadway parade to the Riviera. In Havana, they put me up in luxury. They made me feel like a king, which I was, until payday, that is. We drew 25,000 into their new sports palace but when it came time for the payoff, Castro took 20 percent off the top and the rest of the money was processed through a Canadian bank. It took me a month to get my do-re-mi, so I'll be staying in the good ol' United States from now on."

"He's a marvel," said matchmaker George Linnehan. "He's the fastest big man in the game. He was such an attraction at the Chicago Amphitheater that the promoters had to move outdoors into the Chicago White Sox ballpark."

In April 1960, two of the most popular wrestlers in the world matched up at Madison Square Garden—Haystacks Calhoun and Bruno Sammartino. The crowd didn't know who to root for. Late in the match, Haystacks had Sammartino caught in a headlock, but Sammartino reached around, grabbed Calhoun's legs, and slammed him to the mat. Sammartino had become the first wrestler to slam Haystacks Calhoun.

Calhoun takes down Bruno Sammartino in March 1961 at Madison Square Garden in New York City.

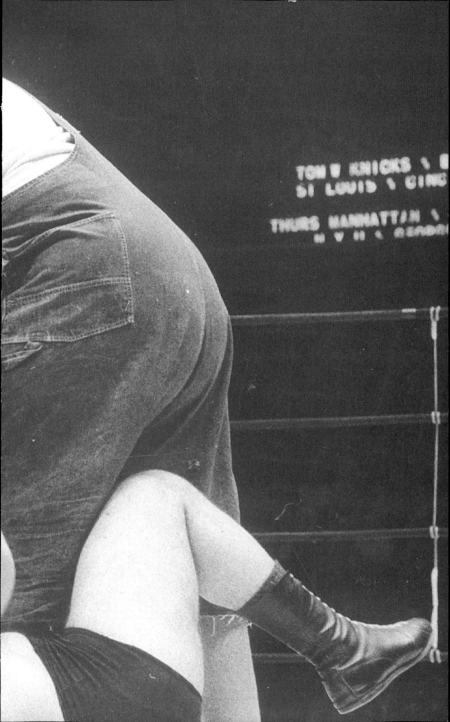

"I'm glad some-body finally did it," Haystacks said after-ward. "It kind of takes the pressure off, like a baseball pitcher going into the late innings with a no-hit game going for him. When they finally get a hit off him, he feels relieved."

"Haystacks is a wonderful fellow," said Sammartino. "I hope he didn't mind me lifting him."

Fred **Blassie** runs away from **Haystacks** to avoid being slammed by the weighty wrestler.

Haystacks beat wrestling villain Fred Blassie in what was considered by the experts to be a tremendous upset. He brutalized Blassie, twisting his neck and then bloodying him with his king-sized belt. By the middle of 1960, Haystacks was making $100,000 a year. The public couldn't get enough of him. Haystacks drew a record wrestling crowd for a card at Griffith Stadium in Washington. He wrestled Killer Kowalski and drew another record crowd. On July 29, 1960, he drew 30,000 fans to Comiskey Park in Chicago for a match against Bruno Sammartino. The gate— the total amount of money paid by fans for tickets—was $89,000, the largest in the city's wrestling history.

Amazingly, Haystacks wasn't the biggest wrestler on the circuit. In 1961, he wrestled Happy Humphrey, who weighed 750 pounds. The sight of these two giants in the ring was astounding. They weighed a combined 1,350 pounds! The ring could barely hold their imposing bulk. In fact, before the card, the ring had been specially reinforced with plywood two-by-fours so it wouldn't collapse.

Haystacks had a big advantage over Humphrey. Although he was 150 pounds lighter, he was much faster and much more agile. Humphrey could barely drag his huge body across the ring. Calhoun moved with the agility of a 250-pounder.

The crowd got what it paid for. The building shook when Humphrey and Haystacks bumped bellies in the middle of the ring. The fans gasped in shock when, in an astounding feat of strength, Haystacks lifted Humphrey and slammed him to the mat. Haystacks won the match, and later the two men became close friends. After all, they had a lot in common.

Meanwhile, doctors kept insisting that Haystacks's weight posed a health risk. At an annual checkup, a doctor told Haystacks that his weight was putting too much strain on his heart.

"You might not live out the year," the doctor warned Haystacks. "Either give up eating or give up wrestling."

In a real-life clash of the titans, Haystacks tussles with 750-pound Happy Humphrey in 1961.

These words scared the life out of him. And to make things worse, a few weeks earlier, Happy Humphrey had died of a heart attack.

Haystacks couldn't give up wrestling. A couple of weeks earlier, McMahon had given him his first match at Madison Square Garden against "Kangaroo" Al Costello, a member of the famous and hated Fabulous Kangaroos from Australia. Haystacks had made it to the big time. He had worked too long to stop now.

Instead, he went on a diet. But he didn't lose weight. Instead, Haystacks lost energy. He lost matches he ordinarily would have won easily. He would get exhausted after only five minutes in the ring. Realizing this, Haystacks's opponents would stay away from him for the first five minutes or until he was tired. Then they'd move in and win. Finally, frustrated by losing, Haystacks gave up his diet.

The doctors turned out to be wrong. At the end of the year, Haystacks was still alive. And he was showing no signs of slowing down.

A Weighty Problem 6

His size also worked against Haystacks. According to the rules, he could never be champion. In many states, wrestlers over 300 pounds were not allowed to participate in championship matches.

Another rule was that a champion couldn't wrestle an opponent twice his size. Because of this, Haystacks was always hoping and waiting for a 350-pound champion to come along. But Haystacks was a good sport, and he never complained. The fame was good, and the money was even better. He could easily afford breakfasts of a dozen eggs, a loaf of bread, and a quart of milk. Life on the road was lonely, and he missed his wife, Honey Bird, but he had the life that he had always dreamed of.

Haystacks and Bruno Sammartino had several more spectacular matches. They battled in a series of thirty-minute time limit draws. Sammartino marveled at the fact that a man as big as Haystacks could last thirty minutes in the ring. Late in one match, much to the crowd's amazement, Haystacks monkeyflipped Sammartino to the mat.

"He was the first man I met who was as strong as me," said Sammartino, who in 1963 would win the World Wide Wrestling Federation heavyweight title and hold on to the belt for eight years. "The only men I've seen as strong as him have been Yukon Eric and Ivan Koloff."

Fred Blassie knew all about Haystacks's tremendous strength. One night in Milwaukee, Wisconsin, Blassie was scheduled to meet three opponents in the main event. Shortly before the match, the promoter found out that one of the three couldn't make the match. Instead of having Blassie wrestle the remaining two, the promoter matched him up against Haystacks.

Blassie was cruel, vicious, and relentless. He blinded Haystacks with a series of illegal eye gouges and then shoved him out of the ring and onto the floor. Haystacks climbed back into the ring, caught Blassie in a stranglehold, then tried to crush him to death. The referee tried to restrain Haystacks, but he couldn't. Finally, Haystacks was disqualified. The referee and several other men pulled Haystacks off Blassie. The crowd cheered for Haystacks and booed Blassie.

"Next time you match me with three guys, stick to your bargain," Blassie told the promoter, "and if they don't show up, I'll take on any five normal guys in the house. As for Calhoun . . ."

He had nothing else to say.

Haystacks continued to take on the most violent men in the sport. He wrestled the Sheik, who had won thirty-three consecutive matches at Maple Leaf Gardens in Toronto. During their match, Haystacks had the Sheik on the canvas and was about to deliver his splash when referee Tiger Tasker (who had been the referee for each of the Sheik's victories at the Gardens) disqualified Calhoun. Apparently, the referee had called for a break and Calhoun had not complied. Furious, Calhoun pushed the referee and delivered the splash anyway.

The Sheik's body convulsed as he crashed to the mat. Four men carried

Haystacks Calhoun and his tag team partner Yukon Eric prevail over the Sheik and the Bruiser in Cincinnati.

him back to the locker room. Haystacks had ended the Sheik's winning streak in one minute, forty-two seconds. Again, the crowd cheered for Haystacks. In fact, crowds always cheered for this lovable big man who seemingly never had a bad word to say about anyone.

"After a match, the average wrestler can put on his street clothes and get lost in the crowd," Haystacks said. "But not me. I'm so big I'm always in the public eye. So I try to be careful how I behave, particularly in front of kids. So many adults, particularly athletes, ignore kids. I cater to them, which is why they love me. Kids look up to athletes, and I try to be nice to them and set them a good example. If I drink or cuss or carry on in public, I'm not setting a good example, am I?

"Wrestling gives me both respect and a position in life. I can't hold anything against it. If there's anything wrong with it, I haven't seen it. All of us work hard, take our knocks, and do our best. I've found that most of the people in wrestling are decent."

Easy for Haystacks to say. At his size, he had no reason to break the rules.

"Actually, all I have to do is rough my opponent up a bit," he said. "No matter who I wrestle, it only takes a bit here and a bit there, not to mention my giant splash, and I am the winner. So why should I cheat?"

"I remember one night, the ring caved in and all the people could see of

Haystacks Calhoun and Magnificent Maurice shake hands during their 1965 matchup in New York City.

me was my head and shoulders," Haystacks told the *Charlotte News* in 1962. "I was body slamming a fellow when it happened, so I just kept right on slamming him. All the spectators could see of him was an occasional glimpse of his feet."

Haystacks was defying the odds. He was a big man who couldn't be stopped.

International Hero 7

In 1963, Haystacks made the longest plane trip of his life and ended up in a place where the fans showered him with more love than ever—Japan. Wrestling has always been extremely popular in Japan, where the sport is second only to baseball. Although not many wrestlers have what it takes to become accepted by the knowledgeable Japanese fans, those who do are treated like members of a royal family.

Big wrestlers are well respected in Japan. Because of this, when Haystacks got off the plane, he was greeted at the airport by more than 3,000 people. In Japan, Haystacks's matches attracted sell-out crowds. Fans followed him everywhere he went.

However, when he returned to the United States, Haystacks got a different kind of greeting—from the Internal Revenue Service (IRS). On his tax returns, Haystacks had been claiming food and travel expenses of $50 a day. The IRS insisted he limit his expenses on food to $20 a day. "I can't survive on snacks," Haystacks told the IRS.

Finally, Haystacks invited the IRS guys to join him at a restaurant. They watched in amazement as Haystacks ate a huge meal, consisting of several main courses. They agreed that $20 a day wasn't enough to feed a 650-pound man.

Although his professional life was great, Haystacks was having trouble with his personal life. In 1965, he and his second wife got divorced. After the divorce, he missed the companionship of a woman, and he missed his daughter, too. He rarely made it home to his ranch in Tucumcari, New Mexico. His second wife and daughter lived in Tucumcari, too, but he hardly got to see them. Although he was one of the most popular wrestlers in the world, Haystacks had few friends. Even at the height of his professional success, he felt like an outcast.

"My size has made me a lonely man," he said. "Being the heaviest wrestler in the United States has its drawbacks. Every opponent wants to upset you. Somehow, when they meet me they have more fire than when they wrestle each other. I suppose it's the extra incentive I inspire in them. Whatever it is, I can't afford to relax in there against anybody."

By the very nature of what he was doing, Haystacks was separating himself from other people. He frequently wrestled two or three men at the same time.

"And I win 'em all," Haystacks said in a magazine interview. "But on the other hand, I'd hate to wrestle two or three top wrestlers. I'm confident I can take any one of the top wrestlers in the business today. But two of the top men would be rough. I think it would be mere luck if I defeated two top men at the same time."

Haystacks had no shortage of challengers. And although he had more than proven his ability to defend himself, opponents kept insulting him. It hurt him that so many people could see him only as a fat man. Take Rocky Montero, for example. For weeks in 1968, Montero had been insulting Haystacks and calling him "fat man." When they wrestled at the Olympic Auditorium in Los Angeles, Haystacks tore into Montero. He slammed him violently to the mat, sat on him, and then splashed him for the pin.

Meanwhile, doctors continued telling Haystacks to lose weight, and he kept on defying their pessimistic predictions.

In addition, wrestling promoters kept refusing to grant Haystacks title shots. Even at age thirty-four, at the height of his popularity, Haystacks remained what he had always been—the added attraction.

One of the most famous matches of the 1960s occurred in August 1969 at Boston Garden. Haystacks wrestled Gorilla Monsoon, who weighed 480 pounds. During the match, Haystacks got mad when Monsoon tried to gouge his eyes. When Haystacks appealed to the referee, Monsoon deposited his size-fourteen shoe into Haystacks's belly. Haystacks stumbled backward. While falling backward, Haystacks grabbed his horseshoe. He

Haystacks made Rocky Montero pay for his insults when the two wrestlers faced off in Los Angeles in 1968.

chased after Monsoon with the horseshoe. Monsoon jumped out of the ring.

"C'mon, git up here," Haystacks told Monsoon, who pleaded with the referee to make Haystacks put the chained horseshoe away. When Haystacks wouldn't put it away, the referee started counting. Haystacks dared Monsoon to reenter the ring, but when the referee reached twenty, he raised Monsoon's hand. Haystacks had lost by disqualification.

"I don't know how they could let it happen," Haystacks said. "They let that Monsoon do everything to me. Everybody knows I seldom lose my temper, but this was different. I swear I could have beaten Monsoon to a pulp. It was one of the few times in my life I can remember being disqualified. I shouldn't have been disqualified. Gorilla Monsoon should have been thrown out."

In 1970, Haystacks was teamed with 625-pound Man Mountain Mike at the Cow Palace in San Francisco, California. Their opponents were Mr. Saito and Kinji Shibuya, the world tag team champions. Saito and Shibuya planned to take the tag belts back to Japan, and Haystacks didn't want that to happen.

"Calhoun and Mike are just soft fat boys," Shibuya said, making the same mistake so many other wrestlers had made by insulting Haystacks. "No talent, no skills. We'll prove Japanese wrestlers are much superior to Americans. Japanese masters are better at everything."

At the Cow Palace, the crowd was waving American flags. Saito and Shibuya carried the Japanese flag into the ring. The crowd booed, and then the bell rang. Saito hit Haystacks in the jaw. Haystacks turned to the crowd and said, "I intend to wrestle the American way—cleanly!" Haystacks placed Saito in a headlock, but Saito broke the hold by karate-chopping Haystacks below the belt.

Haystacks doubled up in pain. Saito kicked him in the face. Haystacks escaped a pin attempt, then grabbed Saito in a bear hug. Seconds later, Haystacks pinned Saito to win the first fall.

Saito and Shibuya won the second fall. When the third fall started, the champions were exhausted and resorted to dirty tricks. Saito grabbed Haystacks's horseshoe and beat him over the head. Haystacks fell to the mat, almost unconscious. He was bleeding from the head. The referee had no choice but to stop the match and disqualify the Japanese. Without a deciding pin, Saito and Shibuya retained their belts. Enraged, Haystacks and Man Mountain Mike chased after Saito and Shibuya, and crushed them with a pair of arena-shaking big splashes.

"And we'll win the championship the next time we get 'em,'" Haystacks vowed.

"There will be no next time," Saito said.

And there wasn't.

8 Nothing Fancy— Just Haystacks

There were times when he was lonely. There were times when he felt like an outcast. But Haystacks Calhoun would have never exchanged his life for anybody else's.

In the early 1970s, Haystacks had married his third wife, a woman he described as "a nice southern girl who knows how to prepare simple, home-cooked food."

"We don't go for anything fancy," Haystacks continued. "After a wrestling match, I like a four-pound steak, salad, and fresh vegetables. You know, something like a bowl of potatoes, a bowl of beans, and a bowl of carrots. If the match is something extra hard, like a battle royal, I'll have two steaks."

Haystacks earned $11,000 for winning a twenty-two-man battle royal at Olympic Auditorium in Los Angeles. He had never lost a battle royal until one in 1972 in Los Angeles. Haystacks stood in the middle of the ring by himself while the other wrestlers battled around him. They didn't want to go near him, knowing he could easily eliminate any one of them. Bruno

Sammartino won the match, but only after a dozen men teamed up on Haystacks. It took nine men to pin him. There was no way they could throw him over the ropes.

Haystacks appeared on TV shows with Marty Allen and Merv Griffin, two of the biggest talk show stars of the time. Later, in 1972, he considered retiring, but he was talked out of it by doctors. Retiring, they felt, posed a health risk.

"Because of his size, Haystacks faces a lifetime of exercise," said Dr. Harry Kleinman of the New York State Athletic Commission. "This man can never really retire from an active physical life the way other athletes can. If he did, fat would rapidly form around his heart and much of his

Haystacks is momentarily subdued by a headlock applied by Man Mountain Mike in Los Angeles in November 1974.

muscles would go soft. Calhoun has excess flesh in only one area. That is in the middle front of his torso. Everywhere else, Calhoun is as solid as a rock."

On May 30, 1973, Haystacks realized a dream when he teamed with Tony Garea to win the WWF world tag team championship. It was the first and only world championship of Haystacks's career. They beat Professor Tanaka and Mr. Fuji in Hamburg, Pennsylvania, and held the belt for over three months. Because of the weight restrictions, however, the world heavyweight singles title remained out of Haystacks's reach. What he did have—and what he would always have—was the love and respect of the fans.

Haystacks during a bloody match with Bobby Duncum in New York in 1974.

Despite his size and strength, Haystacks was never brash or pushy.

"You'll see a lot of wrestlers strutting around and shouting," Haystacks said. "I don't go in for that. I don't want to brag or be pushy. With my size, if I did that, I'd really be obnoxious. I'm just an ol' country boy. And I want to stay plain and humble. People wouldn't come to see me if I was a bully and a braggart."

Haystacks Calhoun never changed. He always remained humble and respectful of those who had helped him throughout his career. Haystacks returned to Texas upon his retirement in the late 1970s. This time, the doctors were right. Haystacks's inactivity did him in. He suffered from diabetes as a result of his weight. He died on December 7, 1989, at North Texas Medical Center.

Glossary

armlock Wrestling move where the attacking wrestler pulls his or her opponent's arm behind the opponent's back by placing his or her own arm between the opponent's arm and back.

battle royal Wrestling match where many wrestlers—sometimes twenty or more—fight in the ring at the same time. The object is to eliminate your opponents by dumping them over the top rope and to the floor, one by one. The winner is the last person remaining.

card List of matches on a wrestling show.

chores Tasks or duties done around the house or yard.

countout A wrestler is counted out if he or she is out of the ring for twenty seconds or more. When the wrestler leaves the ring, the referee begins his or her count at one. If the wrestler is counted out, he or she is disqualified.

curfew Prescribed time at which a wrestling card must end. Certain states, such as New York, have had eleven o'clock curfews for wrestling cards.

disqualification   In wrestling, a wrestler can lose by disqualification if he or she uses a foreign object, refuses to obey the referee's orders, breaks the rules repeatedly, is counted out of the ring, or if another person interferes on his or her behalf. Except in the event of a double disqualification (where both wrestlers lose), the victory is awarded to his or her opponent. In most championship matches, the belt does not change hands on a disqualification, only on a pin or submission.

entrée   Main course of a meal.

formidable   Tending to inspire awe or wonder.

handicap   Disadvantage.

headlock   Basic wrestling hold in which the attacker wraps an arm around his or her opponent's head and squeezes.

manager   Person responsible for overseeing a wrestler's activities, both inside and out-side of the ring. Managers often take care of a wrestler's business affairs (such as signing contracts and arranging matches) and also assist with strategy.

pin When either both shoulders or both shoulder blades are held in contact with the mat for three continuous seconds. A pin ends a match.

platoon system In football, the coaching strategy in which players play only offense or defense, but not both.

promoter Person responsible for hiring and contracting the wrestlers for a card or federation. The promoter is also responsible for deciding the matchups for a card.

scuffling Fighting.

tag team Team of two or more wrestlers in a match. One person wrestles at a time. The other wrestler can enter the ring only when tagged by his or her partner.

taunt make fun of.

For More Information

Magazines

Pro Wrestling Illustrated, The Wrestler, Inside Wrestling, Wrestle America, and *Wrestling Superstars*
London Publishing Co.
7002 West Butler Pike
Ambler, PA 19002

WCW Magazine
P.O. Box 420235
Palm Coast, FL 32142-0235
(800) WCW-MAGS (929-6247)

WOW Magazine
McMillen Communications
P.O. Box 500
Missouri City, TX 77459-9904
e-mail: woworder@mcmillencomm.com
Web site: http://www.wowmagazine.com

Web Sites

Professional Wrestling Online Museum
http://www.wrestlingmuseum.com

World Championship Wrestling
http://www.wcw.com

World Wrestling Federation
http://www.wwf.com

For Further Reading

Albano, Lou, and Bert Sugar. *The Complete Idiot's Guide to Pro Wrestling*. New York: Alpha Books, 1999.

Cohen, Daniel. *Wrestling Renegades: An In-Depth Look at Today's Superstars of Pro Wrestling*. New York: Pocket Books, 1999.

Mazer, Sharon. *Professional Wrestling: Sport and Spectacle*. Jackson, MS: University Press of Mississippi, 1998.

Myers, Robert. *The Professional Wrestling Trivia Book*. Boston, MA: Popular Technology, 1999.

Works Cited

"A Heavy Bet on Haystacks." *Wrestling Revue,* Fall 1960, pp. 67–68.

"Brains Vs. Brawn." *Big Book of Wrestling,* July 1969, pp. 6–8.

Bromberg, Lester. "I'm No Freak." *Wrestling World,* October 1965, pp. 42–45.

Furillo, Bud. "Haystacks Is Holding His Own." *Los Angeles Times,* January 12, 1972.

Green, Ronald. "Problems of Being a
    Haystack." *Charlotte News,* August
    14, 1962, p. A-6

"Haystacks and Iron Mike Do or Die for
    The Glory Of America!" *Inside
Wrestling,* June 1970, pp. 26–29.

"Haystacks Cry? You Must Be Nuts!" *The
    Wrestler,* August 1969, pp. 26–29.

Prater, Jerry. "Haystacks Calhoun: Biggest
    of Them All!" *Wrestling World,*
    August 1964, pp. 19–22.

"The Farm Boy and the Blond." *Boxing
    Illustrated* December 1961, pp. 49–51.

"This Is Your Life Haystacks Calhoun." *The Wrestler,* July 1972, pp. 33–43.

Thompson, Roy. "Whipping Him Is Like Finding a Needle in a Haystack." *Winston Salem Journal and Sentinel,* December 31, 1967, p. A-5.

Willis, Robert D. "My Size Has Made Me a Lonely Man." *Wrestling Confidential,* December 1965, pp. 22–25.

Index

Photo Credits

All photos courtesy of *Pro Wrestling Illustrated*.

Series Design and Layout

Geri Giordano